DISCARD
FCPL discards materials that are outdated and in poor condition. In order to make room for current, in-demand materials, underused materials are offered for public sale.

21st Century Skills INNOVATION LIBRARY

Unofficial GUIDES

APEX LEGENDS: Equipment

CHERRY LAKE PUBLISHING • ANN ARBOR, MICHIGAN

by Josh Gregory

CHERRY LAKE PRESS

Published in the United States of America by Cherry Lake Publishing
Ann Arbor, Michigan
www.cherrylakepublishing.com

Reading Adviser: Marla Conn MS, Ed., Literacy specialist, Read-Ability, Inc.

Copyright ©2020 by Cherry Lake Publishing
All rights reserved. No part of this book may be reproduced or utilized in any form or by any means without written permission from the publisher.

Library of Congress Cataloging-in-Publication Data has been filed and is available at catalog.loc.gov

Cherry Lake Publishing would like to acknowledge the work of the Partnership for 21st Century Learning, a Network of Battelle for Kids. Please visit http://www.battelleforkids.org/networks/p21 for more information.

Printed in the United States of America
Corporate Graphics

21st Century Skills INNOVATION LIBRARY

Contents

Chapter 1	**Gathering Your Gear**	**4**
Chapter 2	**Wild Weapons**	**10**
Chapter 3	**Adding On**	**18**
Chapter 4	**Defensive Measures**	**24**

Glossary	**30**
Find Out More	**31**
Index	**32**
About the Author	**32**

UNOFFICIAL GUIDES

Chapter 1

Gathering Your Gear

Have you tried *Apex Legends* yet? This action-packed battle royale game has attracted millions of dedicated fans since it was released in early 2019. At the start of each *Apex Legends* match, players do not have any weapons or other gear to help them survive. Instead, they must search the game's

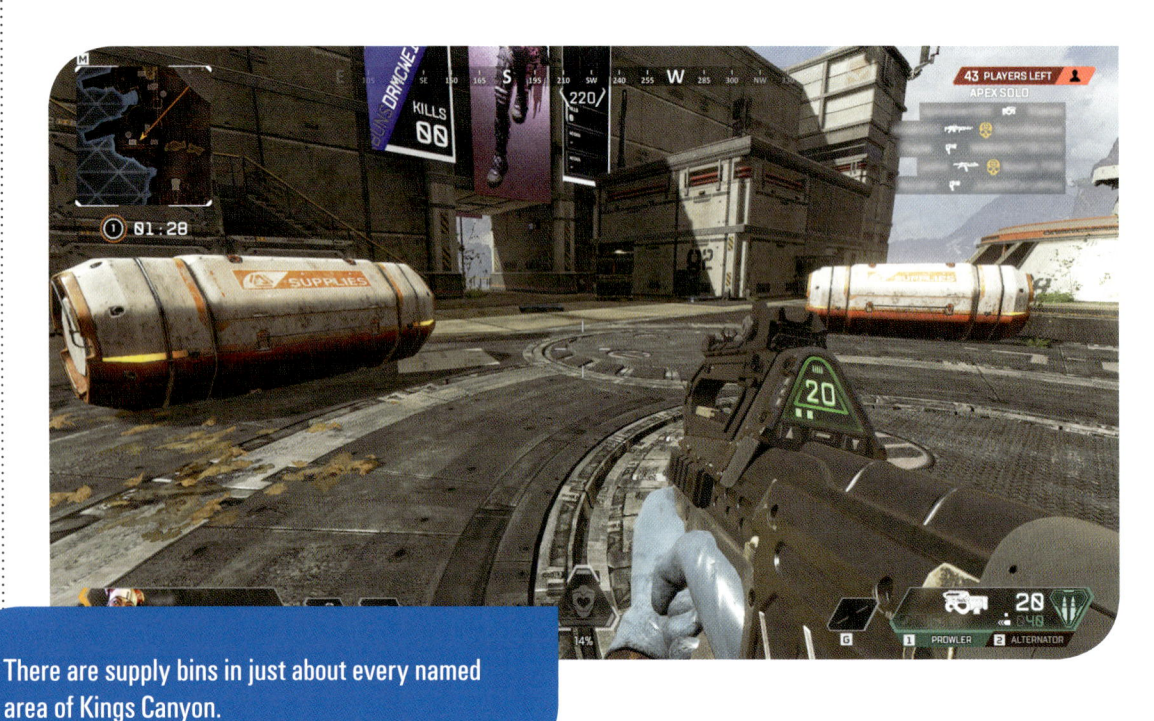

There are supply bins in just about every named area of Kings Canyon.

map, called Kings Canyon, to find everything they need.

Seeking out some basic gear should be your first goal in every match of *Apex Legends*. This process begins with deciding where to land. At the start of an *Apex* match, your team will be aboard a flying ship that travels above Kings Canyon in a straight line. One member of your team will be randomly chosen as the jumpmaster. This player decides when the team should leap from the ship and in which direction it should go while skydiving. This decision can affect the outcome of the entire match, so it is important to choose carefully.

Wherever you choose to land, there will likely be plenty of items near you. Some will be scattered around on the ground, usually inside of buildings or other structures. You will also notice large metal containers called supply bins scattered around Kings Canyon. You can open these to find all kinds of items inside. Supply bins are found in the same locations in every match you play. However, their contents will always be different. This means you can't count on finding specific gear, so you'll have to learn to make do with whatever you can **scavenge**.

UNOFFICIAL GUIDES

Rare Finds

As you gather gear, you might notice that different items in *Apex* are color-coded. Target any item before picking it up to reveal its color and other useful information. These colors are more than just looks. They give you a good idea of how powerful an item is. Each color represents a different level of rarity. In order, they are:

- White (Common)
- Blue (Rare)
- Purple (Epic)
- Gold (Legendary)

The rarer an item is, the better it is compared to other items of the same type. If you have a white body shield, for example, you should look for a blue or purple one to replace it. The game will not let you downgrade by replacing one item for a more common version, so don't worry about dropping a great item by mistake.

In each match, a certain area of the map will be selected as a Hot Zone. In a Hot Zone, you have a chance of finding the very best equipment *Apex* has to offer. You can see where the Hot Zone is by opening your map and looking for the area highlighted with a blue circle. The potential rewards of the Hot Zone always draw a lot of players, so competition is fierce.

You never know exactly what you'll find inside of a Supply Drop.

If you land in a Hot Zone, you might even get knocked out before you've had the chance to pick up a single item. But with plenty of skill and a little luck, you'll make it through and wind up with a backpack full of powerful gear.

Hot Zones aren't the only places to find high-level loot. You will get notifications from time to time when a Supply Drop is about to land. A Supply Drop is a container holding three high-level items that drops from the sky. Its location will be marked on everyone's map, so any players in the area will usually rush toward it. Others might hide nearby and attack unsuspecting

7

UNOFFICIAL GUIDES

players who approach the Supply Drop. But as usual in *Apex*, the rewards are usually worth the risk. Just be careful and stay on guard as you approach a Supply Drop.

Another great place to find powerful equipment is the Supply Ship. You will probably see one of these flying across the map as you skydive at the beginning of a match. Many players try to dive onto a Supply Ship right away. You can also reach Supply Ships from the ground by riding zip lines.

The Supply Ship is an extremely popular spot to land at the start of any match, so be careful.

APEX LEGENDS: Equipment

As you explore Kings Canyon, you might also be lucky enough to come across a Loot Tick. These are small robots that look like the Apex Packs you can open in the game's main menu to unlock **skins** and other rewards. They are usually found in out-of-the-way areas such as on the roofs of tall buildings or tucked beneath staircases. When you see one, smash it to reveal some high-level gear.

As you collect items and prepare yourself with the right gear to take on your opponents, don't forget that *Apex* is all about teamwork. Be sure to share the items you find with your teammates. If you find a good item that you can't use, use the ping feature to let your teammates know its location. Teammates can also use the ping system to let each other know which kinds of items they are looking for.

One of the most fun parts of *Apex Legends* is trying out all of the different Legends. Each character has a different set of unique abilities. However, they can all use all of the same items. This means you are never held back from using certain gear based on which Legend you choose. Feel free to play as whichever character you like!

UNOFFICIAL GUIDES

Chapter 2

Wild Weapons

The most important decision you need to make about your equipment in *Apex Legends* is which weapons to use. Some weapons are simply more powerful than others. Some should only be used if you can't find anything else. But for the most part, each

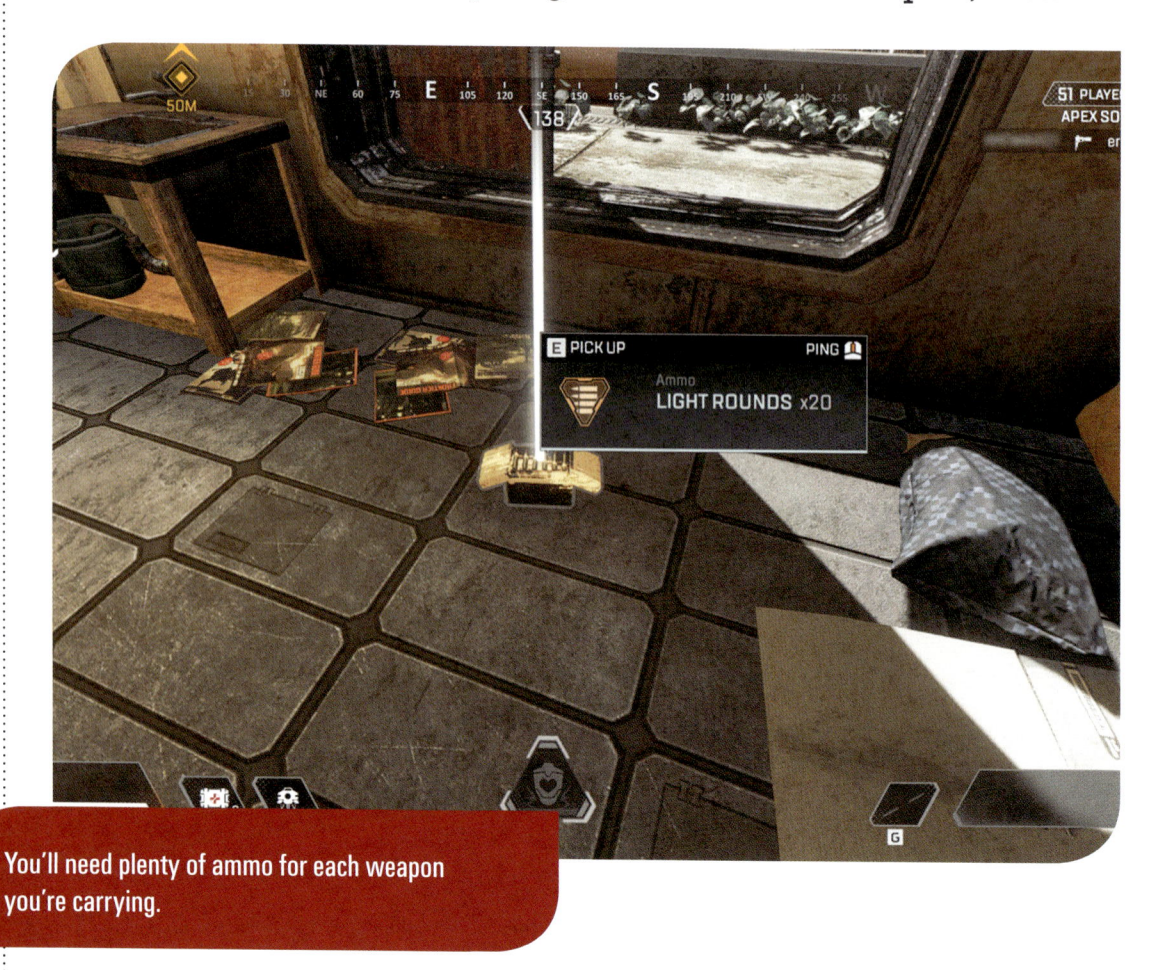

You'll need plenty of ammo for each weapon you're carrying.

one is useful in its own way. Which ones you decide to carry will usually depend on your play style and your team's strategies. And you might not find your preferred weapons in every match, so you should get familiar with all of them. You don't want to be caught in a heated battle with a weapon you don't know how to use.

You will also need to make sure you carry plenty of ammo for your weapons. There are four types of ammo in the game. Each weapon uses just one of the four types, and none of the others will work. Thankfully, weapons and ammo are color-coded, so it is very easy to see which kinds of ammo work with which weapons. The four ammo types are:

- Heavy Ammo (Orange)
- Light Ammo (Green)
- Energy Ammo (Yellow)
- Shells (Red)

The weapons in *Apex Legends* are organized into six main categories: assault rifles, submachine guns, light machine guns, sniper rifles, shotguns, and pistols. The weapons within each category share some basic similarities, but they are not all equal. They might use different ammo types, fire at different rates, or do different amounts of damage.

Assault rifles are generally good all-around weapons. They are fairly effective at any range and pretty easy to use. There are four of them to choose from. The Havoc uses energy ammo, while the Flatline and Hemlock use light ammo. The R-301 relies on heavy ammo.

Submachine guns, or SMGs, work best at close range. They tend to fire quickly, but lack **accuracy**. There are three to choose from. The Alternator and R-99 use light ammo, while the powerful Prowler requires heavy ammo.

Light machine guns are powerful, but slow to start firing. They can do a lot of damage if you catch an enemy by surprise or jump into a fight that is already going on. However, they are less effective when you are the one being caught off guard. There are just two light machine guns in the game. The Devotion uses energy ammo, and the Spitfire takes heavy ammo.

Sniper rifles are the perfect long-distance weapons. They have incredible range and are very accurate. Each shot does a lot of damage. However,

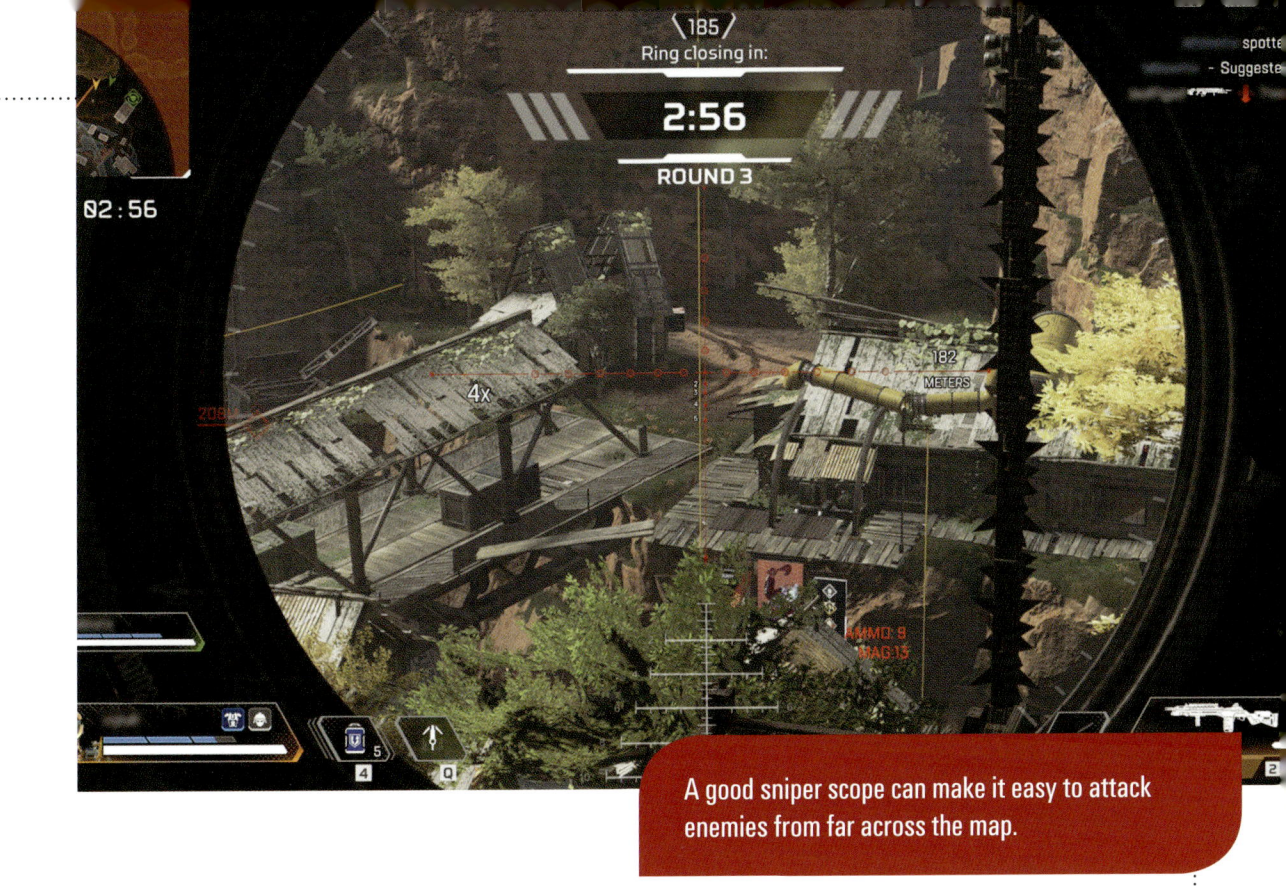

A good sniper scope can make it easy to attack enemies from far across the map.

they are very slow. There will be a pause between each shot. The **magazine** size for sniper rifles is very low, and reloading takes some time. There are four sniper rifles in *Apex Legends*. The Longbow uses heavy ammo, the G7 Scout uses light ammo, and the Triple Take uses energy ammo. The fourth sniper rifle, the Kraber, is very special. It is one of just two gold legendary weapons in the game. This weapon is extremely powerful and accurate. It comes with a very strong scope. The downside is that it does not use any of the standard ammo types in the game. Instead,

UNOFFICIAL GUIDES

it comes with eight rounds of its own special ammo. Once you have fired all eight shots, you won't be able to reload.

Shotguns are the most powerful weapons at close range. If you are not great at pinpoint aiming, these are the perfect weapons for you. Each shot covers a wide area, so even if you don't hit an enemy straight on, you will likely still do some damage. There are four

A few well-aimed shotgun blasts can take out an enemy faster than most other weapons.

APEX LEGENDS: Equipment

Throwing Weapons

In addition to your two main weapons, you can also carry several small, throwable weapons. Frag grenades are basic explosives. When you throw one, it will explode four seconds later. Its explosion is fairly powerful, especially if an enemy gets caught right in the middle of the blast.

Thermite grenades explode as soon as they hit something, whether it's a wall or another player. The explosion creates a wall of fire that can cause damage to your enemies over time.

Finally, there is the arc star. This throwing star can stick to enemies. It causes damage when it hits. Three seconds later, it explodes in a burst of energy. This can knock out an enemy's shields and cause additional damage. It can also briefly stun anyone caught in the explosion.

shotguns in *Apex Legends*. Three of them, the EVA-8 Auto, the Peacekeeper, and the Mozambique, use shell ammo. The fourth is the game's other gold legendary weapon. Like the Kraber sniper rifle, this weapon uses its own special ammo and can't be reloaded once you run out. Called the Mastiff, it comes with 20 shots. Each one is incredibly powerful, so if you use them right, you won't need more.

The last weapon category is pistols. These small weapons might not seem like the most fun

UNOFFICIAL GUIDES

The RE-45 can come in handy if you're a good shot, but it is not the most powerful weapon.

or powerful choices at first, but you might be surprised at how effective they can be. The P2020 and RE-45 both use light rounds. They fire quickly and are fairly accurate, making them useful in a variety of situations. The Wingman fires heavy ammo. Its magazine only holds four shots, but each one is very powerful. The Wingman is also highly accurate. These things add up to make it one of the best weapons in the game.

Which weapons you decide to carry depends entirely on your personal preferences and skill level.

The very best players can win fights no matter which weapons they and their enemies have. There are a few things you should always keep in mind, though. First, you can only carry two weapons at a time. This means you should choose two that go well together. If you want to use a light machine gun, consider grabbing a pistol or shotgun as well. This will ensure you can react quickly and fire back right away if someone attacks you. If you're carrying a sniper rifle, be sure to also pick up something that is useful at closer range. You will likely lose every time if you try to use your sniper rifle up close.

Also, some weapons are simply not very good compared to other options. For example, most players agree that the Mozambique shotgun and P2020 pistol are very weak. If these are the first weapons you find, go ahead and grab them. Any weapon is better than nothing. But you will probably want to be on the lookout for better choices as soon as you can find them. Of course, you might find that you like these weapons. If this is the case, don't be afraid to use them just because other players disagree!

UNOFFICIAL GUIDES

Chapter 3

Adding On

Almost every weapon you pick up in *Apex Legends* can be modified and improved in different ways by finding items called attachments. You'll find these all over the place, mixed in with weapons and other loot. Attachments can increase your weapon's magazine size, allow your scope to

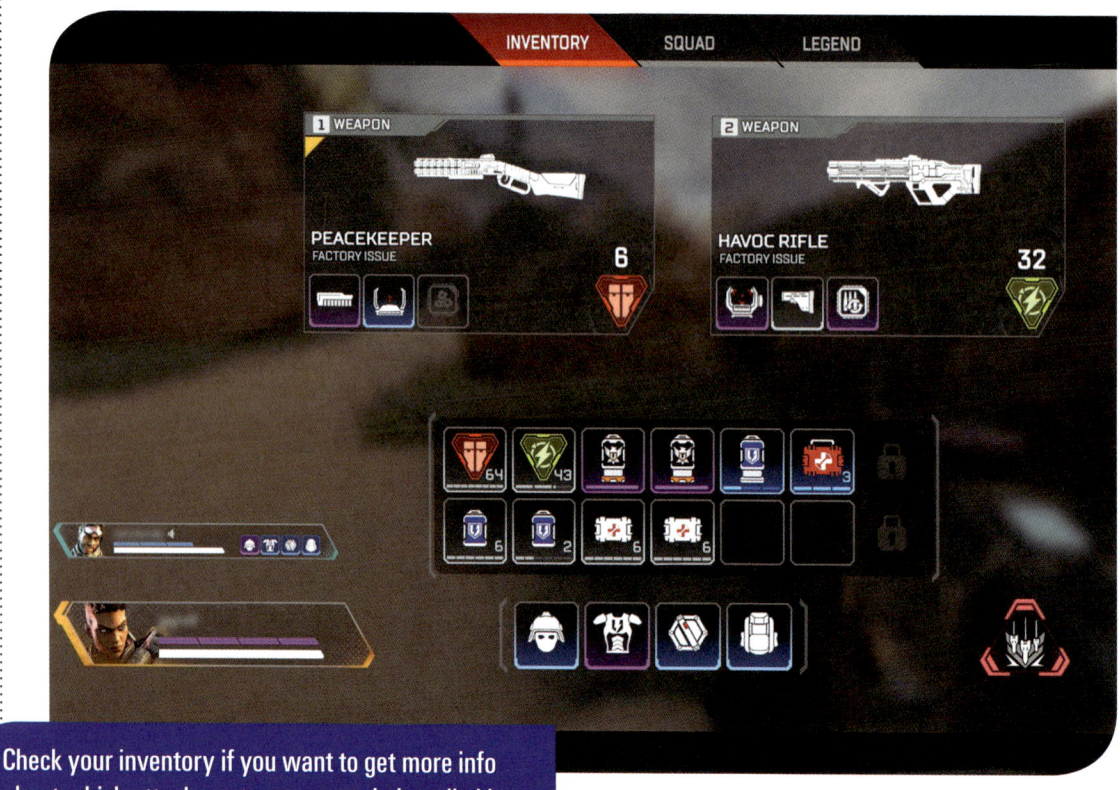

> Check your inventory if you want to get more info about which attachments are currently installed in your weapons.

18

APEX LEGENDS: Equipment

zoom in closer, and much more. Except for the two gold legendary weapons, each weapon has two to five attachment slots. Each slot will only accept certain types of attachments. Additionally, some attachments will only work with certain types of weapons. For example, you can't put a powerful sniper scope into the **optic** slot on a shotgun.

    This might seem complicated at first. However, it will all make sense the more you play the game. When you aim at an attachment before picking it up, a box will pop up showing which kinds of weapons it will work with. It will also tell you whether or not you have a weapon that can accept the attachment. Finally, it will tell you if you already have a different attachment equipped. This way, you can decide whether to keep your current attachment or try the new one.

    Pretty much all weapons have an optic slot. This slot allows you to equip attachments dealing with scopes and sights. Some might allow you to zoom in from great distances. Others change the way your weapon's sights work, often making it easier to aim. As mentioned above, some optic attachments only work

UNOFFICIAL GUIDES

on long-range or short-range weapons. Others can be slotted into any weapon.

Mag attachments deal with a weapon's magazine size and firing rate. Some can even reduce the time it takes to reload. Each of these things can make the difference between victory and defeat in a close fight.

Barrel attachments focus entirely on reducing your weapon's recoil. Every time you fire a shot, your aim

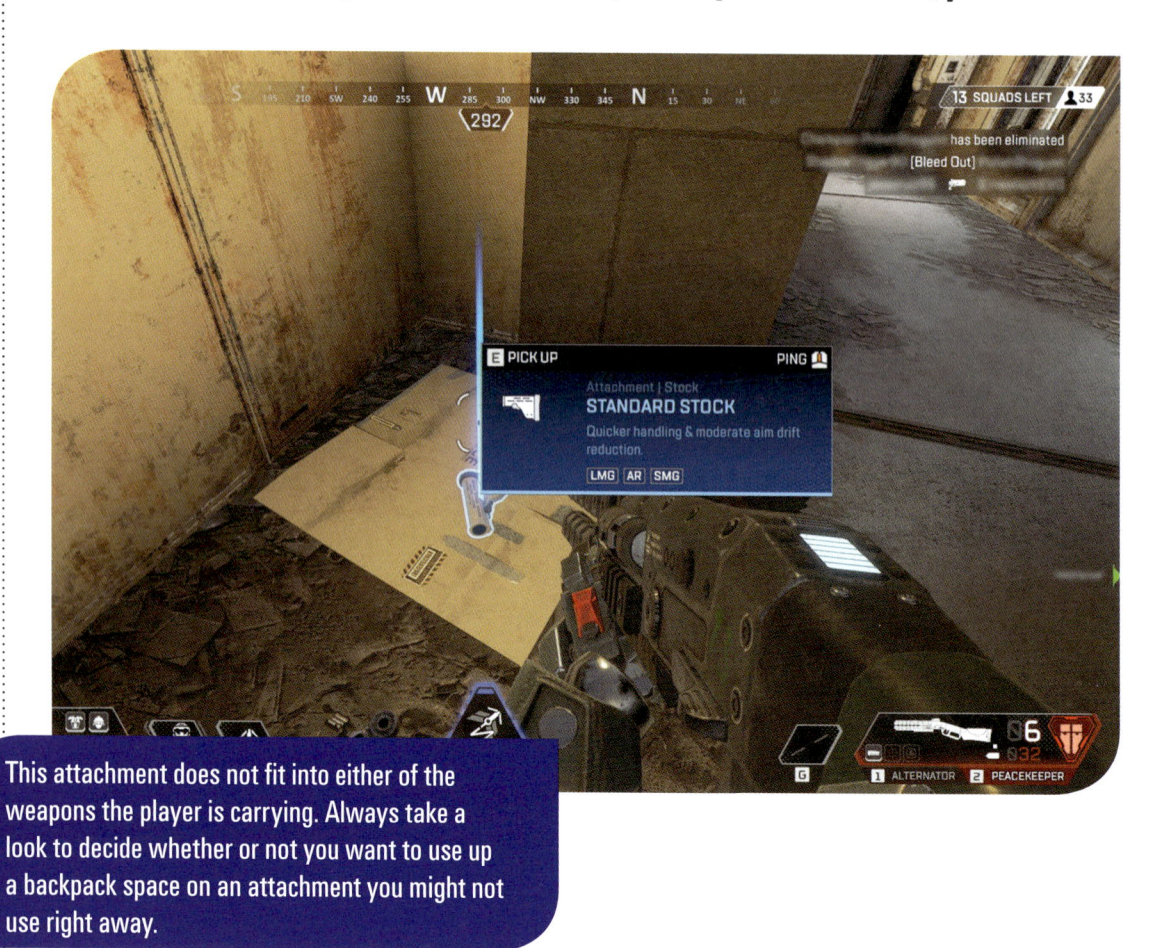

This attachment does not fit into either of the weapons the player is carrying. Always take a look to decide whether or not you want to use up a backpack space on an attachment you might not use right away.

APEX LEGENDS: Equipment

Managing Your Attachments

When you pick up a new weapon to replace one you are currently holding, the game will show you whether any of your current attachments will work with the new weapon. It will then automatically transfer them to the new weapon when you pick it up. This means you don't have to spend time messing around in the **inventory** screen.

Remember that you can only equip an attachment to one weapon at a time. Also, you can pick up attachments even if you don't have the right weapons to match them. They will simply sit in your backpack until you pick up the right weapon. This is very useful if you find a great attachment early in a match.

will jump in a certain direction. For some weapons, this jump can be drastic. If you simply keep firing, your aim will be way off after a few shots. Barrel attachments reduce the distance your aim jumps with each shot. With a good one equipped, your weapons will be much more accurate.

Stock attachments reduce the time it takes to aim down your weapon's sight or scope. They also help keep your aim from swaying back and forth while you are looking down the sight or scope. In other words, they give you a steadier aim. This is especially important at long distances, where being slightly off on your aim can be the difference between a hit and a miss.

UNOFFICIAL GUIDES

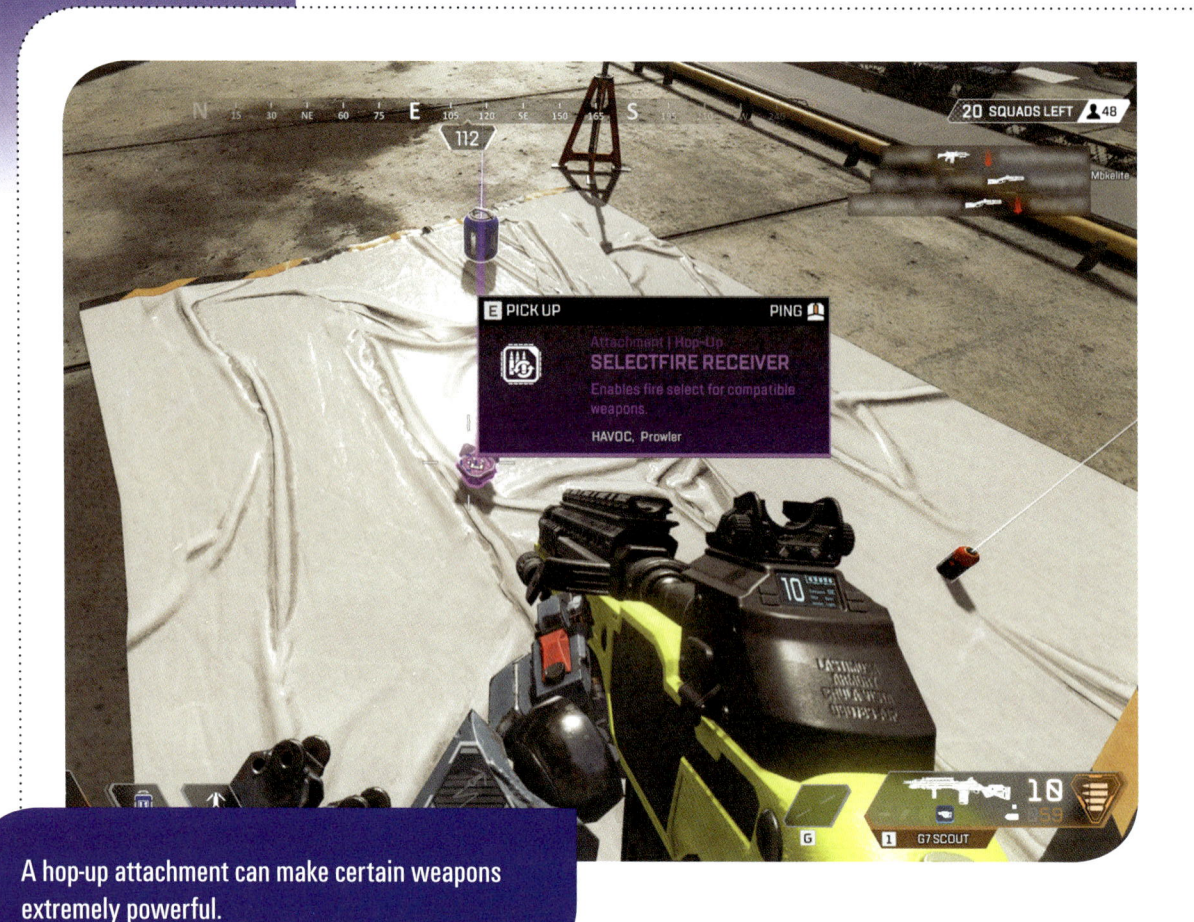

A hop-up attachment can make certain weapons extremely powerful.

Finally, there are attachments called hop-ups. These are some of the best attachments you can find. There are four different ones, and each only works with two specific weapons. Hop-ups offer very specific bonuses, and they can completely change how useful a weapon is. For example, the Devotion light machine gun and Havoc assault rifle both require you to hold down the fire button for a little while before they actually start firing. But there is a hop-up attachment called a Turbocharger. Adding it to either of these weapons will allow them to start firing as soon as you press the button.

If you find purple or gold attachments, they are likely to be better than the more common white and blue versions. But other than that, attachments are mostly a matter of personal preference. Use what you can find and what feels best to you.

UNOFFICIAL GUIDES

Chapter 4

Defensive Measures

Not every piece of equipment you pick up in *Apex Legends* is used to attack other players. You will also need a variety of defensive and healing gear if you want to succeed.

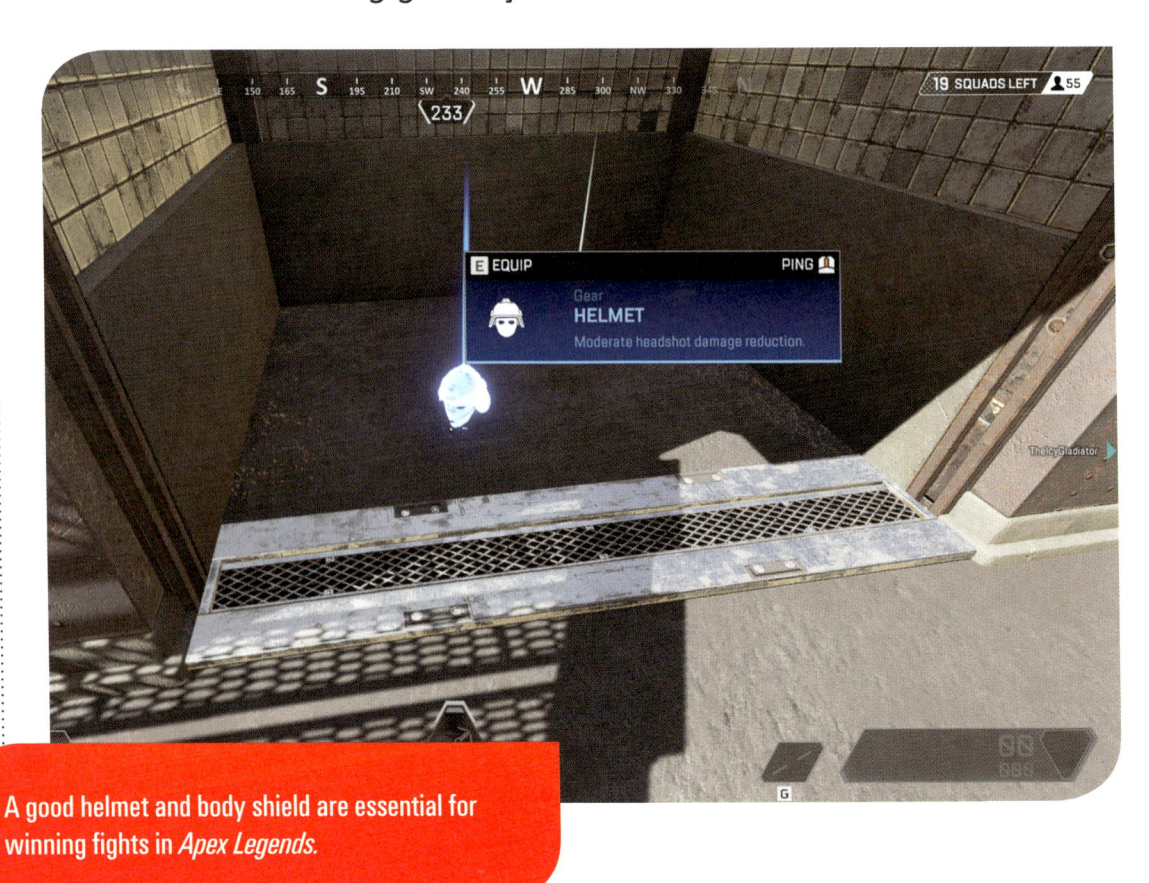

A good helmet and body shield are essential for winning fights in *Apex Legends*.

24

APEX LEGENDS: Equipment

When you are seeking out items at the beginning of a match, always keep an eye out for shields. Shields will reduce the amount of damage you take. This will allow you to last longer in battles.

There are three main types of shields. Body shields work by adding extra protection on top of your health points. Your body shield must be reduced to zero before you lose any health points. Like many other items in the game, body shields come in white, blue, purple, and gold varieties. Rarer versions always offer more protection than the more common versions. Always be looking for an upgrade.

You can also equip a helmet. Helmets reduce the amount of damage you take when an enemy's shots hit you in the head. Normally, headshots do a lot more damage than shots to other parts of your character's body. This means a helmet can really come in handy.

The last type of shield is called a knockdown shield. This is a special device that only comes into play when your character is knocked down. If you have a knockdown shield when this happens, you can activate it to give yourself some extra protection while you wait for a teammate to **revive** you.

UNOFFICIAL GUIDES

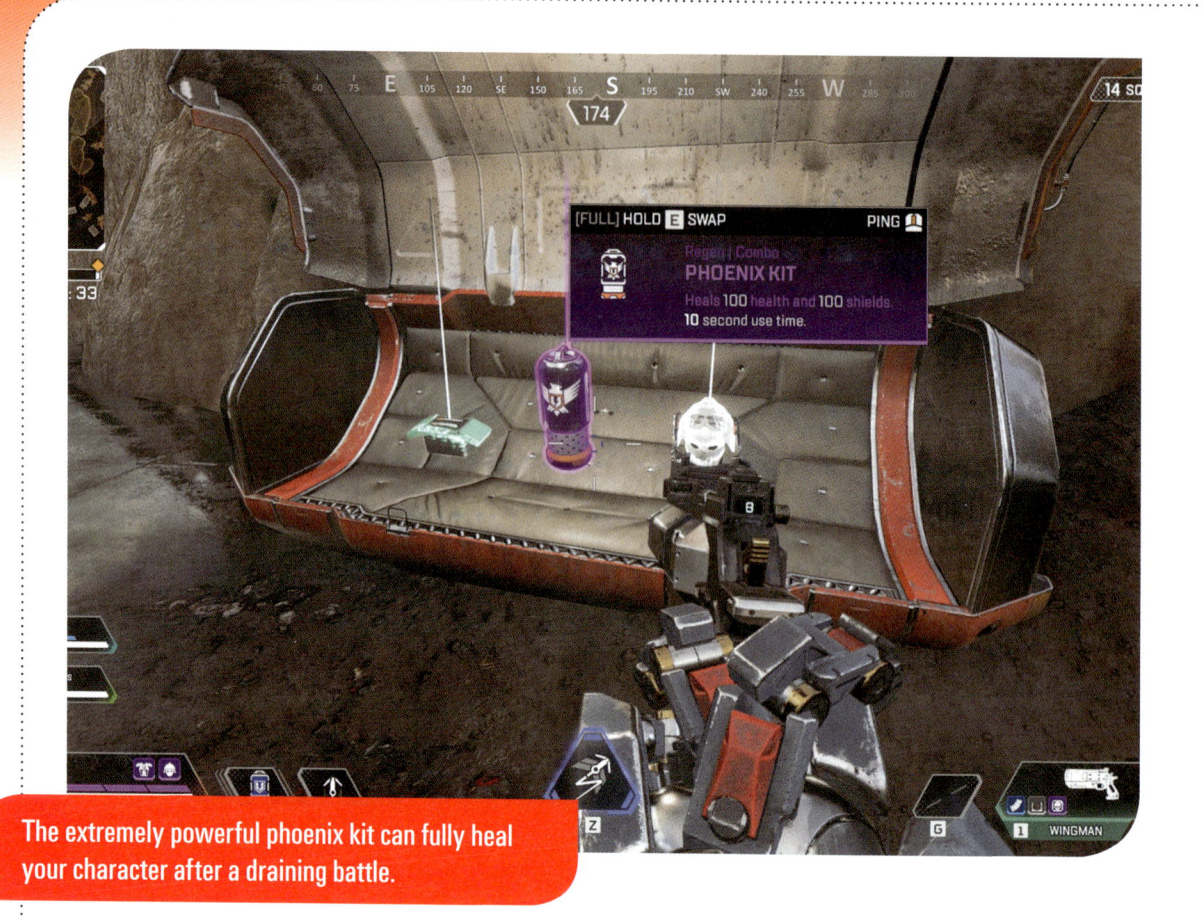

The extremely powerful phoenix kit can fully heal your character after a draining battle.

Even if you are really good at *Apex Legends*, you are bound to take damage from time to time. In these cases, you can use items to restore your shields and health points. Each healing item takes a few seconds to use. During this time, you cannot attack. Be sure you are in a safe place before you try to heal.

Syringes are the most basic healing items. They restore 25 health points and take 5 seconds to use. Medkits are more powerful. They restore 100 health

APEX LEGENDS: Equipment

Changing with the Times

Like many online games, *Apex Legends* is always growing and changing. The game's developers regularly release **patches**. Sometimes patches are used to fix bugs or add new features to the game. They can also be used to adjust the game's balance. For example, the developers might decide that a certain weapon is too powerful, giving an unfair advantage to players who find it. They might change the game to make the weapon weaker or harder to find. This would make the game fairer to all players.

Because *Apex Legends* can change at any time, you might have to adjust your strategies and learn new things from time to time. If you come to depend too much on a specific weapon or piece of gear, a single patch could make the game a lot harder for you. If this happens, keep practicing. You're sure to find a new play style that works for you.

points at a time. However, they take a full 8 seconds to use.

Shield cells and shield batteries restore damage to your body shield. Cells restore 25 points in 3 seconds, while batteries restore 100 points in 5 seconds.

If you have a lot of damage to both your health and shields, a phoenix kit is just what you need. This item gives you 100 shield points and 100 health points. It takes 10 seconds to use, though, so be careful.

UNOFFICIAL GUIDES

One final piece of equipment to look out for as you play is a backpack upgrade. At the start of a match, you have eight spaces in your inventory. Backpack upgrades can increase this up to a total of 14 spaces. This will allow you to carry more ammo, healing items, and other useful gear. Like shields, you can only equip

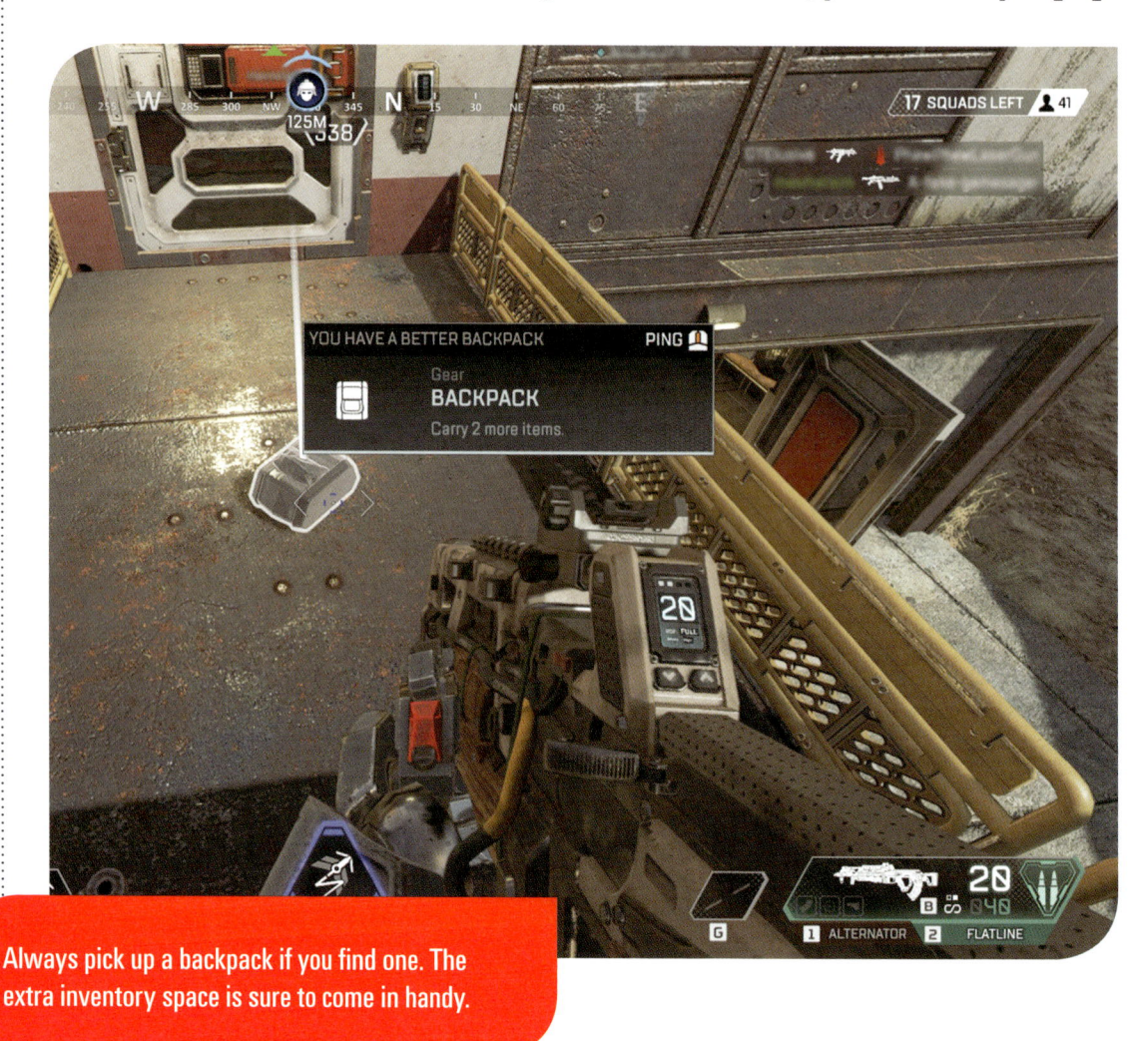

Always pick up a backpack if you find one. The extra inventory space is sure to come in handy.

one backpack upgrade at a time. If you want more spaces, you'll need rarer versions of the upgrade.

By now, you should be familiar with pretty much all the items you can find in *Apex Legends*. It is up to you to decide how you'll put your equipment to use. It's time to grab some friends, head out to the canyon, and start practicing. Good luck!

Glossary

accuracy (AK-yuh-ruh-see) a measurement of how close to a target something is

inventory (IN-vuhn-toh-ree) a list of the items your character is carrying

magazine (MAG-uh-zine) a container that holds a certain amount of ammo to be used in a weapon

optic (OP-tik) relating to vision

patches (PATCH-is) downloadable updates for a video game or other software

revive (rih-VIYV) to bring back to life

scavenge (SKAV-uhnj) to search for useful items

skins (SKINZ) different appearances your character can take on in a video game

Find Out More

BOOKS

Cunningham, Kevin. *Video Game Designer*. Ann Arbor, Michigan: Cherry Lake Publishing, 2016.

Powell, Marie. *Asking Questions About Video Games*. Ann Arbor, Michigan: Cherry Lake Publishing, 2016.

WEBSITES

Apex Legends
www.ea.com/games/apex-legends
Check out the official *Apex Legends* website.

Apex Legends Wiki
https://apexlegends.gamepedia.com/Apex_Legends_Wiki
This fan-made website offers up-to-date information on the latest additions to *Apex Legends*.

Index

ammo, 11, 12, 13, 14, 15, 16
arc star, 15
assault rifles, 11, 12, 22
attachments, 18–23

backpack upgrades, 28–29
barrel attachments, 20–21
body shields, 6, 25, 27

color-coding, 6, 11, 23

developers, 27

grenades, 15

healing items, 26
helmets, 25

hop-ups, 22–23
Hot Zones, 6–7

inventory, 28–29

knockdown shields, 25

landing areas, 5, 7
legendary weapons, 13, 15, 19
light machine guns, 11, 12, 17, 22
Loot Ticks, 9

mag attachments, 20

optic attachments, 19–20

phoenix kits, 27
pistols, 11, 15–16, 17

rare items, 6–7, 9, 25, 29

shield batteries, 27
shield cells, 27
shields, 6, 15, 25–26, 27
shotguns, 11, 14–15, 17, 19
skins, 9
sniper rifles, 11, 12–14, 17, 19
stock attachments, 21
submachine guns (SMGs), 11, 12
supply bins, 5
Supply Drops, 7–8
Supply Ship, 8

throwable weapons, 15

About the Author

Josh Gregory is the author of more than 150 books for kids. He has written about everything from animals to technology to history. A graduate of the University of Missouri–Columbia, he currently lives in Chicago, Illinois.